WILD WONDERINGS

Scientists and their Questions

Cathy Iammartino, Director of Publications and Digital Initiatives

PRINTING AND PRODUCTION
Colton Gigot, Senior Production Manager

ART AND DESIGN
Cover and Interior Design and Illustrations by Linda Olliver

PRODUCTION AND PROJECT MANAGEMENT
KTD+ Education Group

National Science Teaching Association
Erika C. Shugart, PhD, Executive Director

405 E. Laburnum Ave., Ste. 3, Richmond, VA 23222
NSTA.org/store
For customer service inquiries, please call 800-277-5300.

28 27 26 25 4 3 2 1

Cover image (top): agrino/Shutterstock

ISBN 978-1-68140-959-7

A catalog record of this book is available from the Library of Congress.

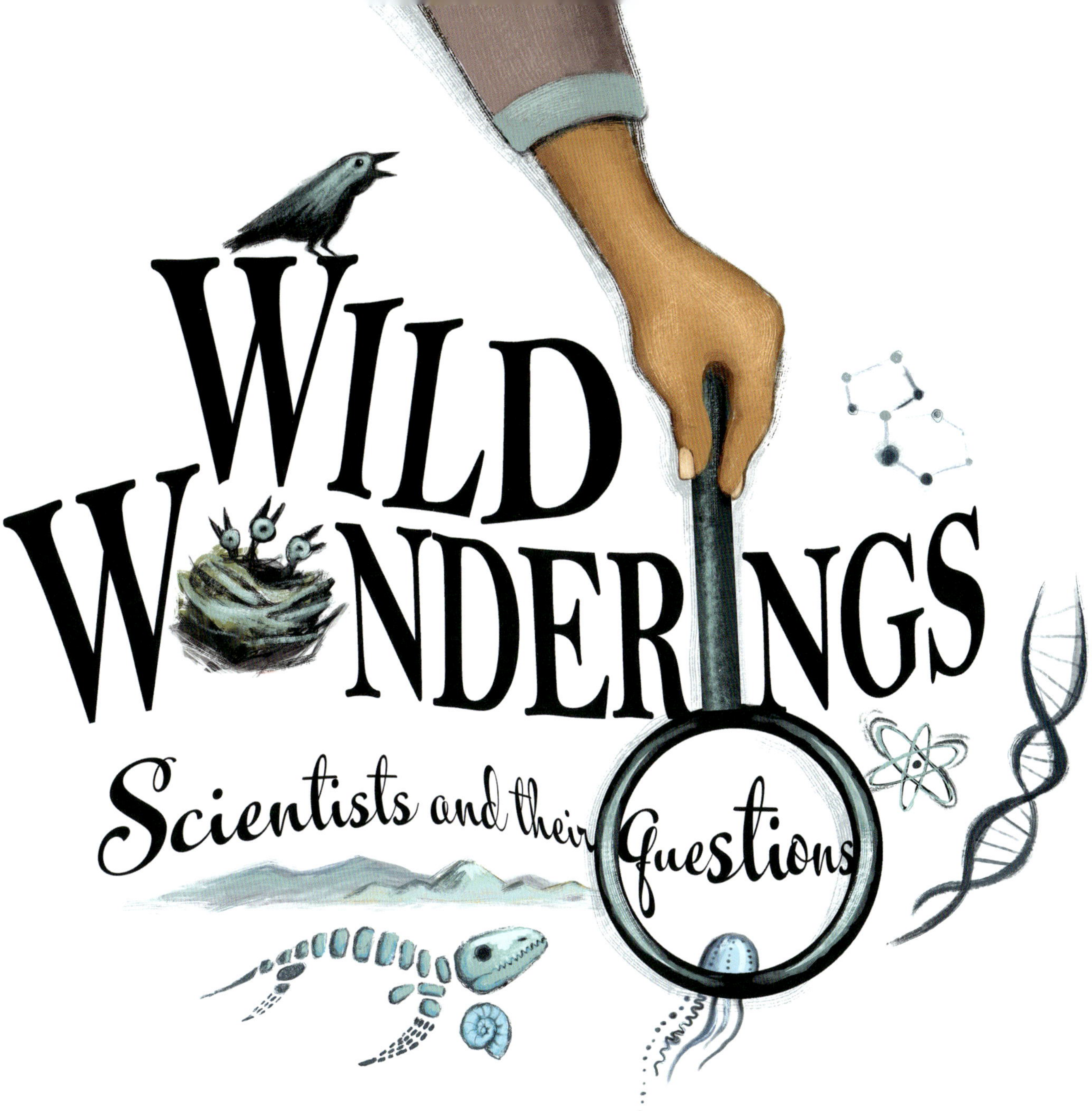

Wild Wonderings

Scientists and their Questions

By Jessica Fries-Gaither

Illustrated by Linda Olliver

Richmond, VA

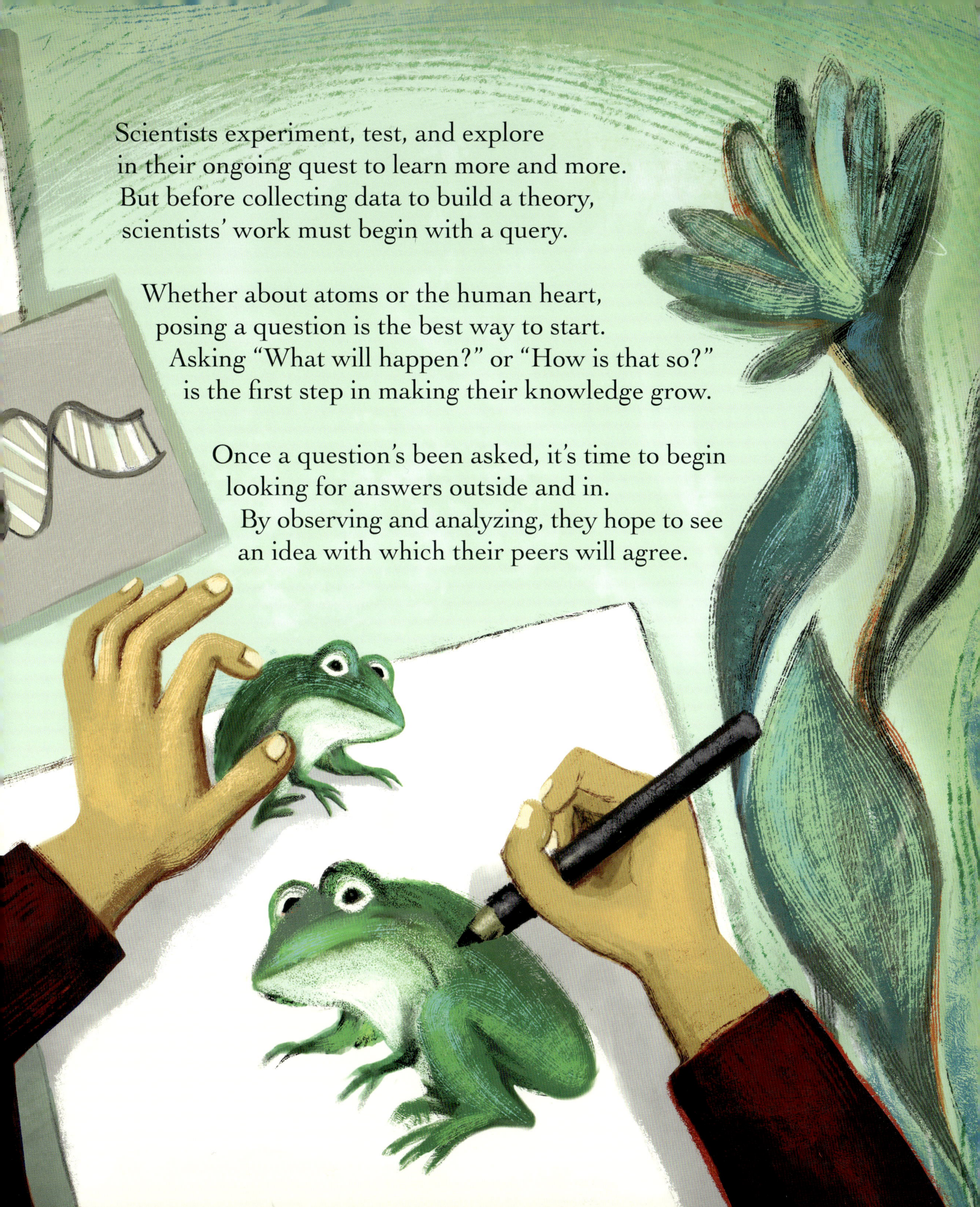

Scientists experiment, test, and explore
in their ongoing quest to learn more and more.
But before collecting data to build a theory,
scientists' work must begin with a query.

Whether about atoms or the human heart,
posing a question is the best way to start.
Asking "What will happen?" or "How is that so?"
is the first step in making their knowledge grow.

Once a question's been asked, it's time to begin
looking for answers outside and in.
By observing and analyzing, they hope to see
an idea with which their peers will agree.

They strive to find answers in every location,
from out in the field to aboard the space station.
But even though they are up to the task,
science can't answer every question they ask.

Scientific questions are those we can test
by collecting data in a way that seems best.
Asking "Who?" or "Why?" can't be answered like this,
but still they are questions we should not dismiss.

Scientists in these pages will help you to see
just how important good questions can be.
Looking back through time shows this to be true:
Their questions have changed the world's point of view.

Thales ["THAY-leez"] of Greece, ahead of his time,
was widely known for his curious mind.
The way he posed questions about a natural event
and answered them set a new precedent.

Why did the Nile River flood every year?
What caused the earthquakes that brought such fear?
Could weather patterns predict a huge crop
or provide warning that the harvest would flop?

While his countrymen looked to the gods,
Thales searched for a natural cause.
His questions and answers paved the way
for the type of science we conduct to this day.

His wild questions showed this to be true:
When you ask, you can think in a way that is new.

What makes it colder the higher you go?
Eunice Foote decided she wanted to know.
Her simple experiment explored the ways
in which gases were heated by the sun's rays.

What did she find when her study was complete?
Carbon dioxide trapped the most heat.
And another question that Ms. Foote asked:
What if Earth's atmosphere had more of that gas?

The conclusion she drew was not a surprise.
More CO_2 would make temperatures rise.
Future studies would prove her correct,
a phenomenon now called "the greenhouse effect."

Her wild questions showed this to be true:
Asking them can cause a breakthrough.

ART. XXXI.—*Circumstances affecting the Heat of the Sun's Rays;* by EUNICE FOOTE.

(Read before the American Association, August 23d, 1856.)

MY investigations have had for their object to determine the different circumstances that affect the thermal action of the rays of light that proceed from the sun.

Several results have been obtained.

First. The action increases with the density of the air, and is diminished as it becomes more rarified.

The experiments were made with an air-pump and two cylindrical receivers of the same size, about four inches in diameter and thirty in length. In each were placed two thermometers, and the air was exhausted from one and condensed in the other. After both had acquired the same temperature they were placed in the sun, side by side, and while the action of the sun's rays rose to 110° in the condensed tube, it attained only 88° in the other. I had no means at hand of measuring the degree of condensation or rarefaction.

The observations taken once in two or three minutes, were as follows:

Exhausted Tube		Condensed Tube.	
In shade.	In sun.	In shade.	In sun.
75	80	75	80
76	82	78	95
80	82	80	100
83	86	82	105
84	88	85	110

This circumstance must affect the power of the sun's rays in different places, and contribute to produce their feeble action on the summits of lofty mountains.

Secondly. The action of the sun's rays was found to be greater in moist than in dry air.

In one of the receivers the air was saturated with moisture—in the other it was dried by the use of chlorid of calcium.

Both were placed in the sun as before and the result was as follows:

Dry Air.		Damp Air.	
In shade.	In sun.	In shade.	In sun.
75	75	75	75
78	88	78	90
82	102	82	106
82	104	82	110
82	105	82	114
88	108	92	120

Did Earth's land look different a long time ago?
An answer Alfred Wegener ["VEY-geh-ner"] wanted to know.
He noticed the shapes of two continents matched.
Could the land masses have once been attached?

Rocks and fossils provided more clues.
Evidence that Alfred could certainly use.
He concluded that all land was once joined as one,
named it Pangaea, and thought his work done.

But even with evidence, he couldn't say how
the continents moved to where they are now.
In the future, new studies would provide
support for his theory that others denied.

His wild questions showed this to be true:
Asking can lead to something brand new.

Pangaea

Alexander Fleming wanted to cure disease.
Many lives were saved thanks to his expertise.
How did he do it? Here is a confession:
An accidental finding led to his question.

His lab was a mess. He left things everywhere,
including a Petri dish out in plain air.
When mold grew on it, there was no denying
that the bacteria in it had started dying.

Was it just a coincidence?
Testing after that day confirmed
that the mold kept bacteria at bay.
The mold made a substance that killed the bad cells,
findings that Fleming's lab notebook retells.

He named it "penicillin," and knew it would be
a remarkable life-saving discovery.
We can treat infections like never before
because of a finding too great to ignore.

Fleming's wild questions
showed this to be true:
Asking leads to findings that
help me and you.

Margaret Nice ["NEES"] is a scientist of great regard
for observing song sparrows in her backyard.
Why do birds sing? At the time, no one knew.
It was a question she chose to pursue.

She tracked individuals by banding their legs,
peered into nests, and counted numbers of eggs.
She concluded that singing was all about space
and keeping an intruder in its rightful place.

Mrs. Nice shared
her findings far and near,
writing about the birds she held dear.
One remarkable thing about what she did:
She did all this at home, while raising her kids.

Her wild questions showed this to be true:
Asking is something anyone can do.

MAP I. *Interpont in the Spring of 1932*

Where did our ancestors live long ago?
Mary Leakey and her husband wanted to know.
Though many believed Asia was the place,
the Leakeys sought to make a different case.

They worked in Africa, digging for bones,
looking for fossils among ancient stones.
Year after year under the blazing hot sun,
searching for evidence of where we'd begun.

Their many discoveries would change the world's mind:
Africa was the cradle of all humankind.
And another find of which many talked:
footprints that showed how our ancestors walked.

Mary's wild questions showed this to be true:
Asking can prove old ideas are untrue.

Stephen Hawking wondered about black holes and space,
thinking through every puzzling case.
He worked not in data, but dabbled in theory,
and created models to answer each query.

Something else that should be addressed:
He suffered from an illness called ALS.
While his body declined, his brain stayed quite keen,
sharing brilliant thoughts through his voice machine.

Dr. Hawking wrote books and appeared on TV,
explaining his models so that others could see.
Audiences were struck by his humor and ease.
His genius wasn't limited by his disease.

His wild questions show this to be true:
Asking provides new paths to pursue.

Patricia Bath was a doctor for eyes.
Her life's work earned her many a prize.
Work in two different neighborhoods led to a question
that helped make her a leader in her profession.

She noticed the rate of blindness wasn't the same
in Black and white neighborhoods; what was to blame?
She uncovered a problem and made others aware:
The difference was simply lack of access to care.

She started a program to address this woe.
She trained volunteers; then out they would go.
With simple exams, volunteers could spot
conditions that were treatable if they were caught.

The vision of thousands was saved in this way.
Community ophthalmology continues today.
By pioneering techniques to improve people's sight,
Dr. Bath ensured that vision is a basic human right.

Her wild questions showed this to be true:
Asking them is the just thing to do.

Long, long ago, a disaster happened worldwide.
Most of Earth's life, including dinosaurs, died.
Adriana Ocampo wondered what all this meant.
What could have caused this extinction event?

One idea was that an asteroid crashed,
filling the sky with huge clouds of ash.
The ash blocked the sun and caused plants to die.
Small and large animals followed suit by and by.

Unfortunately, there was no evidence at hand.
To find it, Dr. Ocampo studied the land.
Observing satellite images, she noticed sinkholes.
Finding a pattern in them was one of her goals.

She led expeditions to the area she found,
and studied the rocks they found in the ground.
They were pieces of asteroid broken off on impact,
the great space rock crumbling on first contact.

Her wild questions showed this to be true:
Asking can help you find a crucial clue.

They're a curious bunch, that much is true.
Asking questions, after all, is what scientists do.
No matter the topic that they have proposed,
their work begins with a question they've posed.

Rosalind Franklin asked questions about DNA,
discovering its shape with a type of X-ray.
Dr. Tarter uses telescopes to look for a trace
of evidence that proves there is life out in space.

Ernest Everett Just was curious about cells,
while Eugenie Clark wondered where a shark dwells.
But questions aren't just for scientists, you see.
You can ask, too! Now what will yours be?

The scientists profiled in this book are a diverse group of men and women who have studied many different branches of science throughout history. Learn a bit more about them here.

Thales of Miletus (c. 624 BC–546 BC) was the first to engage in what is known as scientific philosophy, or investigations into the natural world. Some call him the first scientist in history. Thales (pronounced "THAY-leez") asked questions about natural events such as floods, earthquakes, and eclipses, and he looked for patterns in nature to answer them. While his explanations were not always correct, his work represents an important transition from mythology to scientific explanation.

Eunice Foote (1819–1888) was an American scientist, women's rights campaigner, and inventor. She conducted experiments to determine the effects of the sun's thermal energy on various gases in Earth's atmosphere, including hydrogen, carbon dioxide, and water vapor. This was the earliest experimental work on what we call the greenhouse effect and the earliest discovery of carbon dioxide's role in global warming. John Tyndall presented similar findings three years later and is often incorrectly credited as the one to make this discovery.

Alfred Wegener (1880–1930) was a German scientist who studied astronomy and meteorology. In 1910, he noticed that the coastlines of South America and Africa seemed to fit like pieces in a jigsaw puzzle. Wegener (pronounced "VEY-geh-ner") conducted research, and upon learning that similar fossils and rock formations were present on both continents, proposed that continents had once been joined together in a supercontinent he called Pangaea. However, because he could not explain how continents could move, his ideas were not accepted by the scientific community until the 1960s with the theory of plate tectonics.

Sir Alexander Fleming (1881–1955) was a Scottish physician, pharmacologist, and microbiologist. Serving as a member of the Royal Army Medical Corps during World War I caused him to be interested in antiseptics and preventing infections. He is best known for his discovery of penicillin, a substance produced by Penicillium mold that prevents bacterial growth. Fleming received the Nobel Prize in Medicine in 1945 for this early work in antibiotics. He was knighted for his scientific achievements in 1944.

Margaret Morse Nice (1883–1974) was a renowned American ornithologist despite not holding an official academic position for much of her life. While she earned a master's degree and planned to pursue a PhD, marriage and the pressures of raising a family led her to stay home while her husband worked as a scientist. Determined to continue her research, Nice (pronounced "NEES") tracked the life and behavior of song sparrows in the local area over many years. This type of study had not previously been done, and Nice pioneered techniques for observation, including banding individual birds using brightly colored plastic from children's toys. She published hundreds of papers and several books and contributed important data to the understanding of territorial behavior in birds.

Mary Leakey (1913–1996) was an English paleoanthropologist who made several important discoveries in the field of human evolution. She was an excellent artist, and her skill in drawing led her to working at archaeological digs from an early age. She illustrated a book for archaeologist and anthropologist Louis Leakey in the 1930s. She eventually married Leakey, and the two became a famous scientific team, moving to Tanzania in the 1940s to do research at Olduvai Gorge. There, Leakey discovered an 18-million-year-old skull of a common ancestor of humans and apes, and later, a 3-million-year-old skull of an early human ancestor (now known as Australopithecus boisei). Leakey continued her work after her husband's death, discovering a trail of early human footprints at Laetoli, a site in Tanzania.

Stephen Hawking (1942–2018) was an English theoretical physicist and cosmologist (a scientist concerned with the origin of the universe). Hawking was a professor of mathematics and director of the Centre for Theoretical Cosmology at Cambridge University. His work included investigating the origin of the universe and the nature of black holes. He was also a popular author, writing best-selling books including *A Brief History of Time*. Hawking suffered from ALS (amyotrophic lateral sclerosis), or Lou Gehrig's disease, a disease that gradually paralyzed him. Although he was given two years to live following his diagnosis, he lived with the disease for more than fifty years, getting around in a wheelchair and using a speech-generating device to communicate.

Patricia Bath (1942–2019) was an American ophthalmologist and inventor. After completing medical school, she worked at Harlem Hospital while also pursuing a fellowship at Columbia University. During this time, she noticed that African American patients were twice as likely to suffer from blindness than white patients. Wondering why, she found that lack of access to ophthalmological care in the Black community was the cause. In response, she founded a new discipline known as community ophthalmology, in which volunteers trained as eye workers went out into the community to test vision and screen for threatening eye conditions. This approach has saved the sight of many. Dr. Bath also invented a treatment for cataracts and was the first African American female doctor to receive a medical patent.

Adriana Ocampo (1955–present) is a Colombian planetary geologist at NASA. She discovered evidence for the Chicxulub impact crater in the Yucatán Peninsula of Mexico using satellite images, and has led many expeditions to the area. The Chicxulub crater, named for a nearby town, was formed by an asteroid strike about 65 million years ago. A widely accepted theory is that the changes in climate caused by this asteroid strike led to the extinction of 75% of all animal and plant species on Earth, including all non-avian dinosaurs. While this theory had been proposed earlier, Ocampo's discovery provided important evidence to support it.

You can ask your own questions! Here's how:

1 Observe carefully. Scientists are great observers. They use their senses to closely study objects and events in the world around them. You can do this, too, with a little practice. For example, you might notice some interesting things about the way a toy car moves when you pull it back and let it go.

2 Turn your observations into questions. If you pay close attention to things around you, you'll probably start coming up with questions easily. Sometimes it helps to write these down like this:

I noticed ________________________________,

so I wonder ________________________________.

3 Sort and classify your questions. How might you answer each question?

- Some questions are *research questions*: ones we can answer by reading articles and books, doing online searches, watching videos, or interviewing experts. An example of a research question is "What colors does this car come in?"
- Other questions are *observational*: ones we can answer by using our senses (and sometimes science tools like hand lenses, rulers, and microscopes). An example of an observation question is "What path does the car take when I let it go?"
- Some questions are *testable*: we can do an experiment to find the answer. An example of a testable question is "Will the car go farther if I pull it back farther?"

Sometimes it helps to write questions on sticky notes and group them into categories, as you can see in the pictures below.

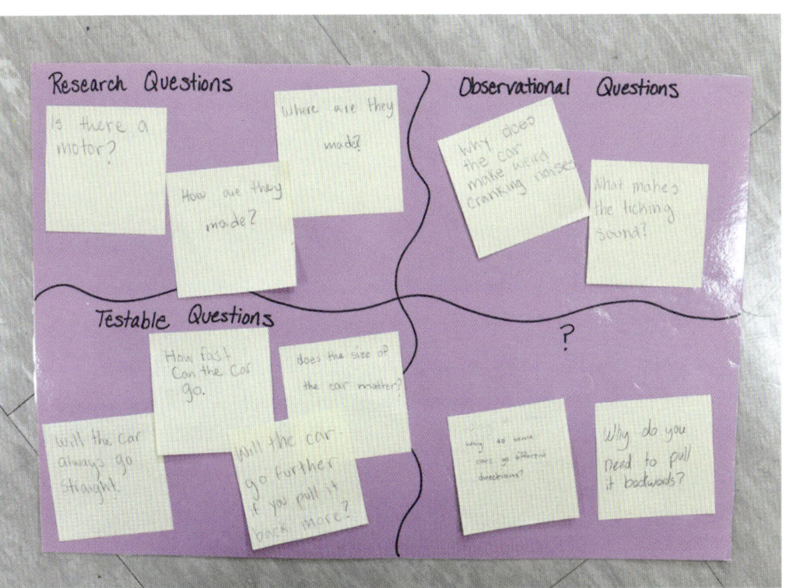

4 Decide which question you want to answer first. How will you find the answer? Will you do research? Will you do an experiment? Don't forget to share what you've learned with others.

The more you practice asking questions, the better questions you'll ask. Make it a habit to ask questions every day!

Image Credits

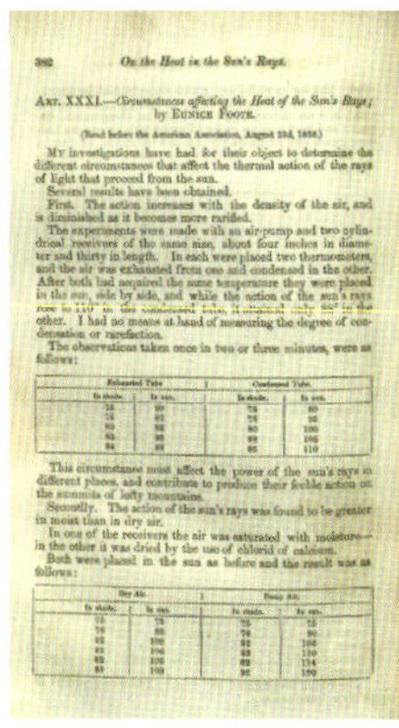

382 On the Heat in the Sun's Rays.

ART. XXXI.—Circumstances affecting the Heat of the Sun's Rays; by EUNICE FOOTE.

(Read before the American Association, August 23d, 1856.)

MY investigations have had for their object to determine the different circumstances that affect the thermal action of the rays of light that proceed from the sun.

Several results have been obtained.

First. The action increases with the density of the air, and is diminished as it becomes more rarified.

The experiments were made with an air-pump and two cylindrical receivers of the same size, about four inches in diameter and thirty in length. In each were placed two thermometers, and the air was exhausted from one and condensed in the other. After both had acquired the same temperature they were placed in the sun, side by side, and while the action of the sun's rays rose to 110° in the condensed tube, it attained only 88° in the other. I had no means at hand of measuring the degree of condensation or rarefaction.

The observations taken once in two or three minutes, were as follows:

Exhausted Tube		Condensed Tube.	
In shade.	In sun.	In shade.	In sun.
[illegible]	[illegible]	[illegible]	[illegible]

This circumstance must affect the power of the sun's rays in different places, and contribute to produce their feeble action on the summits of lofty mountains.

Secondly. The action of the sun's rays was found to be greater in moist than in dry air.

In one of the receivers the air was saturated with moisture—in the other it was dried by the use of chlorid of calcium.

Both were placed in the sun as before and the result was as follows:

Dry Air.		Damp Air.	
In shade.	In sun.	In shade.	In sun.
[illegible]	[illegible]	[illegible]	[illegible]

p. 11: Public domain. Biodiversity Heritage Library. *https://www.biodiversitylibrary.org/item/86348#page/247/mode/1up*. Accessed August 21, 2024

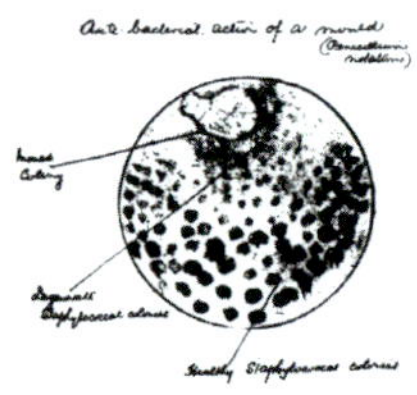

p. 14: Photo courtesy of St. Mary's Hospital Medical School/Science Photo Library.

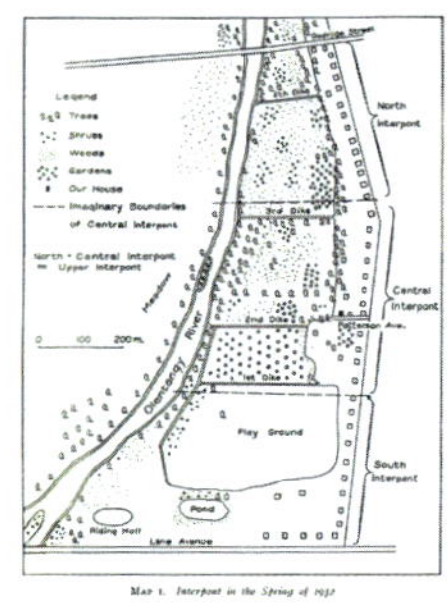

p. 17: Public domain. Nice, M. Morse. (1937). Studies in the Life History of the Song Sparrow [New York]. *https://hdl.handle.net/2027/mdp.39015006891488?urlappend=%3Bseq=29%3Bownerid=13510798895637770-33*. Accessed August 21, 2024.

p. 19: Photo courtesy of John Reader/Science Photo Library.

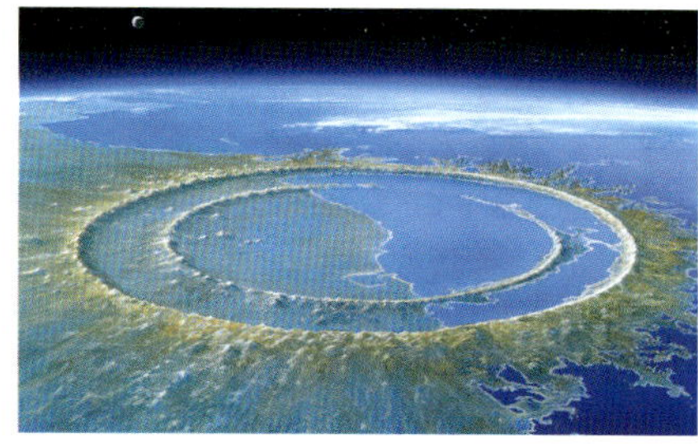

p. 25: Photo courtesy of D. Van Ravenswaay/Science Photo Library.

p. 30-31: Photos courtesy of Bondi Photography, LLC.

About the Author

Jessica is an experienced science educator and an award-winning author of books for students and teachers. Her teaching career began as a middle school math and science teacher in Memphis, TN, through the University of Notre Dame's Alliance for Catholic Education program. She also taught in Anchorage, AK, at the middle school and elementary levels. Additionally, she spent five years in the College of Education and Human Ecology, School of Teaching and Learning at The Ohio State University where she directed NSF-funded projects and provided professional development for elementary and middle school teachers. She is currently the Director of Studies and Lower School Science Specialist at the Columbus School for Girls in Columbus, OH.